[*un*·earth]

[*un*·earth]

Exploring
A Land
With No
Name

Christy Vidrine | Autumn Rogers
Plethora Publishing, Inc.

Published in Waukegan, IL, by Plethora Publishing, Inc.

Unless otherwise indicated, all Scripture quotations are from The Holy Bible, English Standard Version®
Copyright © 2001 by Crossway Bibles, a division of Good News Publishers, All rights reserved.

Scripture taken from the Holy Bible, NEW INTERNATIONAL VERSION®. Copyright © 1973, 1978, 1984 International Bible Society.
All rights reserved throughout the world. Used by permission of International Bible Society.

ISBN 978-0-9802171-1-7

Printed in the United States of America
Library of Congress Control Number: 2008928048

To all sojourners finding their way home.

CONTENTS

TO THE READER

The pages below recount lessons of confusion, peace, struggle, and love within the rich journey that God works in a missional heart. It has been a wild ride for us to get to this point of offering our hearts to you. We are grateful believers in Jesus Christ, who enjoy matchless adventure, unique food, and interesting dialogue with good friends and a game of speed Scrabble. We are young theologians who like to explore the depths of God's word and promises. We want to live exemplary lives of God's illustrious adventure as broken people offering our stories for Him to use any way He desires. After 13 years and a combined 21 short-term mission trips, we have something to say about struggling on the field, questioning God's plan, conflicting with leaders and teammates, and especially the vertigo of re-entry. We know each of our examples will not exactly coincide with yours, however, our hope is you will allow the Lord to write your story in the process of reading ours.

[*un*•earth]

INTRODUCTION

There is a place between each border, a strip of earth; many have come to call the middle land. It is a road, which no one holds allegiance to. It has no name. As I cross from one country to the next, its mystery and barrenness intrigues me and I am left as speechless as the land itself.

I am staring down at the fresh stamp of ink on my passport page. Looking up, I can see the border guard motioning me towards the building in the distance. It is an eerie feeling to walk this ground which holds no language, no flag nor anthem. A piece of land where no one calls home.

So is our time between the mission and Western world. The interim, which is seemingly so short, offers crucial value to the visitor. Your course is determined in this place: everything you are resolved to change, to steward and to live out. In a moment, we will cross into a claimed nation. This transition into 'life as we left it' is challenging, deep and unsettling. Yet hope brims as we unearth the heart of God, processing our time spent overseas and exploring a land with no name.

[*un*•earth]

un•*ea*rth [ən'ər θ]

verb
[trans.] discovering something hidden or lost by
digging, investigation or searching.

[*un*•earth]

14

1

the MIDDLE LAND

I have been on this plane almost 13 hours...most
of the team is asleep. I have sat long enough to
know I need to find my toothbrush and deodorant
fairly soon. I am still a little frustrated the t.v.
screen at my seat does not work. When the first
movie started, I kindly asked the flight attendant
for assistance and she assured me when the
movie was over she would reset the system. Now,
four movies in, I am still trying to decipher the
slanted color silhouettes of my neighbor's screen.
I found myself almost livid when the flight

attendant apologetically informed me I would not be able to watch movies nor was there any other seat I could be moved to. I was upset. I asked for compensation. I am very embarrassed to say I demanded a free international ticket.

After two weeks of relieving famine victims in Kenya, a broken t.v. screen should have been the least of my frustrations. Confined to my two by three foot space, I had plenty of time to reflect on my attitude. Guilt flooded my mind. How could I be so self-absorbed when I had just witnessed the Africans content with so little? It was startling that my resolve to live differently after this experience could dissipate so quickly.

AWARENESS IN THE MIDDLE LAND

It can be challenging to assimilate your overseas experience in the busyness of North American culture. Usually when we return from a mission trip, we return to a whirlwind. Either going back to school, moving to a new place, or seeing our friends and family. This is typical of our Western culture lifestyle: transient, chaotic and fast. We must be aware during this transition, because the story has just begun. It will not matter if you were asking hard questions of God or feeling intimacy with Him while on the field, **if you do not continue the journey once you are home**.

Continuing is the key. Our hope within this chapter is to awaken and invite you to explore the responsibility of your new knowledge. It is common to no longer take the time or discipline to struggle emotionally and reflect spiritually through the process God began in you. In our arrival home from overseas, it is easy to see our radical change waver.

We conform on multiple levels, not only with our experiences on the mission field, but also with our everyday emotions. We often cheat ourselves out of the process of reflection. We boil down the passionate adventure and struggle of life to a few paragraphs on a blog. Our distractions can be as minor as music, food, and movies or as complex as addictions, relationships, and religion - there are plenty of things available to de-sensitize our emotions. The North American culture, by default, offers us many places to run, entertain, numb and comfort. Although other cultures offer some of these distractions, the world of missions usually does not. If you have been in a spiritually charged environment, expect to come face to face with every distraction and addiction when you arrive home. Especially if you return with the expectation to live differently than you were living before. Statistics have shown the level of morality and conviction has fallen drastically among missionaries returning from the mission field. Why is that?

Your trip overseas is an experience typically filled with opportunities of heightened intimacy and interacting with several in need - spiritually, emotionally, or physically. Engaging the powerful beauty of brokenness stimulates an emotional high. When we return home, the heart craves this new intimacy experienced and most are inept to deal with this adjustment. Satan knows we are vulnerable. Destroying this intimacy is his greatest chance at thwarting God's plan. We must be aware.

Engaging in Transformation

As we re-enter the commotion of our culture, the fervor we had overseas becomes significantly muted. The faces of the people who captured our hearts are now pictures on our screensaver. We no longer remember what it is like to wake up in a world of blatant need. We have forgotten the city we live in is also a place filled with lost people. Your process of re-entry is about more than your short-term trip, more than the people you helped and the projects you completed. In coming home, you will see this process entails changing the way you live. It is part of the bigger plan God has to sanctify you as His child. God will continue to weave His lessons from your trip into everyday life.

As uncomfortable as this limbo between worlds can be, we encourage you not to stifle or avoid it. **Transformation has just begun.** Transformation comes as we listen to God and obey His voice. We cannot listen amid a barrage of distractions; we must find a quiet place of silence where we can hear His voice and reflect. This change comes as we embrace His presence in the silent moments and process what He is speaking to us. We must begin to build genuine intimacy.

When we step on foreign soil we are given a place to find God and know Him in a way our culture has not offered. The transition back can either be draining or exhilarating. Stepping into a hectic schedule but holding onto our new learned truths will be a huge challenge. The glorious struggle is for us to find a way to live differently. This is a gift of God's heart, to feel the difference and face it.

So how do you live differently, more healthy after coming home from these experiences? Is it enough to commit one night a year camped out for a cause or attend a mission conference? Do you think God's plan was to cultivate so little in you through this process?

> No, He wants you to be transformed.
> He wants you to live in the tension of His greatness.
> He desires for you to be seasoned with the fire of His presence.

God is relentless when it comes to the ones He loves. He will stop at nothing for your wholeness. Yet we will. We will circumvent the fullness of transformation with something as trite as busyness, excess and lack of discipline.

PRESSING IN DEEPER

At first, I despised the silence I found myself in surrounded by a foreign language. Now, back in America, I crave it. My insecurities, doubts and fears were quieted as I turned my attention to others. Perspective is different here in the

Western world; all I see and all I feel is me. When I was overseas, my map was larger. I could see nothing but their faces, feel nothing but their need. I loved it. We were made to live somewhere in between these two worlds. This glorious struggle teaches us about His grace and how to encounter more healing and wholeness.

There are multiple times you will find yourself in the tensions of re-entry. For our friend Kelsey, her awareness came in the difficulty of returning to her church community. She felt as if no one really understood the experiences she had overseas. Although her church was excited about her trip, their commitment to local outreach left her feeling lonely. For our friend Tim, his experience felt lost even among his friends. Making small talk in regular social settings became trite and frustrating for him. Recognize even your transition back into familiar places could be challenging. Why? **You have changed.** God's plan is to transform you, then offering the "changed you" in these places of familiarity.

Start looking in your everyday life for the things you saw when you were overseas.

Cultivate places of silence and stillness.

Watch for the hurting and the lost.

Look for the simple.

Delve inside your own hurt and loss.

Anything with a soul will capture your attention *if you look deep enough.* Step into the adventure of what you will face as you meet these places of need. The eyes of the homeless and broken are the same in every country, every church, every home, every bar, every tribe, and every university. If our goal is to enter into Him, then this is where we will find Him. He is interlaced throughout each moment. You have arrived home changed, so ask Him again. **Where are You cultivating my influence right now?**

Is it on your campus or in your work place?   *Go deeper.*
Possibly it is in your friendships, in your family?   *Push deeper.*

Maybe in the way you see Christianity, church, or the way you see God?

The battle to press in further into what God is doing is always good.

[*un*•earth]

FOR FURTHER THOUGHT.....

Where is the invitation of ministry in your
neighborhood, your city or on your campus?

Has your view of Christianity, the church, or the
way you see God changed?

[*un*•earth]

g*ra*•p•ple [grapəl]

verb
[intrans.] to engage in a struggle or close
encounter.

[*un*•earth]

2

A *new* MAP

During a summer internship in Malawi, my team and I built a small children's library. One of my favorite parts of the project was painting a map of the world on the outside wall of the building. One afternoon, with a secret plan to spend time alone, I took paint and music out to the library to work on the map. As I was painting the different countries, a scene from the musical "The King and I" flashed into my head. If you have not seen the production, here is a quick synopsis.

Anna, an English widow, has moved with

her son to Siam as a live-in governess. She is responsible to teach the children of the King. Picture a classroom scene. Anna is showing the children a map of the world. The oldest son, heir to the throne, is surprised to see Siam is so little. Having only seen maps of his country, the young prince is confused that Siam is so minor in comparison to the whole world. The prince tells Anna he does not believe her maps are accurate, and becomes very angry with her. He refuses to accept what he has believed all his life is incorrect and the country he will one day rule over as king is so small.

I kept thinking about this scene as I was painting the map in the library. From a different perspective, the whole world does not seem as large as I once thought. Who actually views their own world as small? For us it is all we know. Our culture, friends, church, family, university and career make up our map. Like the prince, we often struggle coming to terms with a world that is bigger than the one we live in. It can be exciting or disappointing to find that our orignal map is not all that there is. Either way, the challenge is taking this realization and applying it to our small corner of the globe. You might get stuck in the revelation of a broadened map. This is normal, but do not allow it to paralyze you. Remember, the goal is to convey what you have learned from the larger perspective to your part of the world.

Knowledge stretches and requires us to expand our belief and to trust the teacher.

Grappling with New Maps

I have been much like the prince with the maps of my own life. My story, my God, my calling and my ministry are huge in my eyes because it is all I like to focus on. God gives me more and more glimpses of the real map with each place I go and culture I see. Often, my response has been questioning His goodness and I find myself angry with Him. I feel tricked or confused.

I thought I was looking at the real map, God. I cannot understand why You would do it this way.

Either God is not the God I want Him to be or His ways are not the ways I think they should be.

God, why do you allow children to be abducted, babies to be left in dumpsters, child sex trade, genocides, and tsunamis?

When we get up the nerve to ask Him these questions something within us breaks. It is in our bold inquiries God invites us into a deeper intimacy and we are released to voice our more personal uncertainties.

God, why would You allow my parent's divorce, my friend's death, or this physical abuse?

What do you really believe about Him in these questions? What truth do you hold to? Answering the question of God's goodness will be the most crucial step in any struggle you encounter.

Lexia shared the story of her life from the stage. She was in tears as she spoke of her birthmother's death and her parent's divorce. As her story grew, she told us about one of the darkest moments of her journey. She had just arrived in a foreign country to do missions when she received a phone call from the home base. Her father had committed suicide the day she left for the mission field. In her tears and anguish, she began to yell, "I have my top button buttoned, I have my top button buttoned!" Lexia had heard a teaching months before about the importance of believing in God's goodness. **Despite all other things, you must know God is good.** It is like buttoning your top button first so that you know your shirt is on straight. You must know God is good in order for your struggle to make a straight path.

> Come; let us return to the Lord.
> For He has *torn us*, that He may *heal us*;
> He has struck us down, and He will

[*un*•earth]

bind us up.
> - Hosea 6:1, emphasis added

Therefore, lift your drooping hands
And strengthen your weak knees
And make straight paths for your feet,
*so that what is lame may not be put out
of joint but rather be healed.*
> -Hebrews 12:12-13, emphasis added

The paradox of these two verses leaves us dumbfounded. The larger map invites us to wrestle with a God who says to trust Him and in the same breath tears us so that He might heal us. This is a crossroad in our relationship with Christ, to take the pain He allows us to endure and either heal from it or to be put out of joint. We must be aware of the battle over our hearts in these times of struggling. As I listened to the faith in Lexia's story, I wonder that if such a test came to me I would have my top button buttoned.

A SEEMINGLY ILLOGICAL GOD

*The space in my mind is too small
for You.*

*The space in my heart is too small
for You too.
And all of the things on this earth
that I've known,
Are too small for all of the greatness
You've shown.*

- Waterdeep

*Oh the glory when He took our
place,
But He took my shoulders and He
shook my face,
And He takes and He takes and He
takes.*

- Sufjan Stevens

These songwriters echo the struggle we all face when our finite minds come into relationship with the Creator. Our paradigms are redefined when we encounter His infinite goodness colliding into a world steeped with pain. When we look at God's bigger map, it is not the map we have always seen or the definition of goodness we have always believed. God takes these opportunities to rewrite our definitions and offer us a view of the wider spectrum.

[*un*•earth]

As we begin to explore these new corners of His map, we find Him in the eyes of an HIV child, in the loneliness of a widow, in the words of life we speak over a malnourished infant and in the prayers lifted up over an un-reached city. If we can believe God is good despite the injustices of a hurting world, we slowly move into believing God is good in the ache of our own broken stories. He is in the midst of your addictions, your brokenness, your tragedies and your struggle. **Only the method of an amazing God would allow our hearts to ache in ways we never thought it could.** He allows it, with the hope that we will engage in a deeper intimacy with our Savior. Sometimes, the Lord offers us Himself without clear answers.

> *I cannot understand the pain, and He replies, Come near to me and I will show you that I understand your questions, and I have pondered them long before you. I have wept bitterly over the injustices of this world, and I have ached as your Father, your Savior, and your Friend.*

FINDING GOD'S HEART IN THE PAIN

Isaiah 5, The Song of the Vineyard is one of my favorite passages. God is moved to write a song for His Son. It is a beautiful invitation for us to see how the Father comforts His Son's broken heart over Israel. God does not change or fix the injustice done; rather He mourns over the loss with Him. Here is how God begins the song,

> *Let me sing for my beloved, my song concerning his vineyard:*
>
> *My beloved had a vineyard on a very fertile hill. He dug it up and cleared it of stones and planted it with the choicest vines. He built a watchtower in it and cut out a winepress as well. What more could I have done for my vineyard than what I had done? When I looked for it to yield grapes, why did it yield wild grapes?*
>
> *- Isaiah 5: 1-2,4*

Picture Jesus working day and night in this

vineyard, His hands are bleeding and dirty from digging. The Father watches the Son give all of Himself to something that He knows will disappoint Him. Yet, at the end of each day, with sore muscles and an achy body, Jesus smiles when He thinks of sharing the outcome of this vineyard with His bride. Jesus is offering all of Himself to build a future with His love, the church. And what does He find?

Wild grapes.
Unfaithfulness.
A broken-heart.

He was broken-hearted over the sin of His prized possession, Israel. The Father was moved as He watched His Son's heart devastated. So moved, that He wrote a song for His Son. In the same way, the great Teacher mourns with us as we wrestle through the unfairness of this world.

We can still find remnants of His broken heart in our relationship with Him today. Yet, God, knowing the outcome, continued to offer the world His best, His love, His Son. Because of sin we live in this broken and painful world. Even today, as we watch the story play out in Christianity, we see the wrong is not erased. We, the bride, continue to produce "wild grapes." On God's larger map, we experience His devotion to us as He stays in the repercussions of our sin. The Lord mourns with us in the pain of this world.

Redemption does not come by the Lord taking away the hurts of His children, but rather in His faithfulness to us in our hurt.

God has been watching His creation for thousands of years now. He has seen the deepest of tragedy, the most painful sin, and has orchestrated the greatest of miracles and a glorious redemption. He has authored it all. The Lord is offering you the opportunity to engage in it with Him; here is your chance to explore the larger map.

[*un*•earth]

FOR FURTHER THOUGHT......

If you wrote today from your experience, how God has broadened your map on this trip, what would you write?

What definitions of His goodness is He redefining in your heart?

If you had all the resources, time and money to make a difference in this world, what would you do?

Now, practically consider what changes you can make to achieve that goal with the resources and relationships in your own corner of the world.

[*un*•earth]

sea•son [ˈsēzən]

verb
[trans.] to render competent through trial and experience; (adj.) battle-scarred, battle-weary.

[*un*•earth]

3

SEASONED *with* FIRE

Something in me exploded, and I lost it. The papers I had been holding were thrown against the wall, I muttered, "I quit" and walked out furiously. And then bawled. Uncontrollably. I felt ignored, exhausted, defeated and under pressure from myself to succeed. The painful hiccups that come from crying were just beginning when the shock set in. My mind was racing.

Did I really just throw something? I stormed out

of my boss's office. Maybe I am fired now! Throwing papers isn't professional. I hate hiccups. I don't want to go back in there. Who will take care of the girls?

After being in the Dominican Republic for over a year, it only took two weeks into a new job position to bring me to this point. I loved the ministry and the teenagers I worked with, but God was not allowing me to be the super-woman I thought everyone needed.

Through different overseas trips and at various stages of my spiritual journey, I come to know myself in new ways. Unfortunately, I am not thrilled when I get a good look inside my heart. God is continually working in me, or better put, moving things out. Anger, anxiety, insecurities, and ultimately pride rise to the surface for me to deal with. It is often in the midst of challenging circumstances and God's accompanying presence that I have felt my weakest. I have to remember weakness does not mean I am less godly; **it is a**

catalyst to greatness.

STAYING IN THE FIRE

> "For everyone will be salted with fire. Salt is good, but if the salt has lost its saltiness, how will you make it salty again? Have salt in yourselves, and be at peace one another."
>
> -Mark 9:49-50

> "Each one's work will become manifest, for the day will disclose it, because it will be revealed by fire, and the fire will test what sort of work each man has done. If any one's work is burned up, he will suffer loss, though he himself will be saved, but only as through fire."
>
> -1 Corinthians 3:13;15

Although these two verses speak of final judgment, they offer insight into God's method of refining us. The fire spoken of is the way God tests our motives and calls forth the heart's true allegiance. This is both comforting and frightening. Comforting, because of the certainty that we will be tested, refined and salted. God will be diligent to see that His children, the salt of the earth, do not lose purpose or flavor. However, the preservative He uses to keep us effective and tasteful is fire. Understanding the promise of judgment, and even more so, the security of God's holy justice will stir a healthy reverence in our work.

Are you facing challenges that are testing your faith and revealing your dedication? The Lord is present in the pain inflicted by others, uncontrollable circumstances and our weaknesses. He is at work to consume everything with His glory. He was with me in the challenges that led me to my boss's office, in all my shortcomings and pride. I was working in my own strength, hoping to impress others and trying to be all the girls needed. It was His grace to orchestrate such fiery circumstances in order to illuminate what I could not see. He met me in my areas of sin to bring me to an attitude of humility. These hardships were allowed so there would be less of me, and more of Him.

A LIVING AND TRUE SACRIFICE

To put it simply, if you have surrendered yourself to live for Christ, you are set ablaze. Just as fire burns and consumes, the presence of the Lord in your life will be a series of refining circumstances. The Holy Spirit will use these to burn away our impurities and engulf our hearts with Him alone. This process of sanctification, becoming more holy, is what salts us, or makes us useful to God and flavorful to the world. Overseas ministry has a way of turning up this fire. If you are malleable, He utilizes everything, from the team dynamics you have to the injustices you witness. All these situations will take you deeper into a heart more like His. You are given the opportunity to learn more about being a living sacrifice. God is a faithful teacher; He will meet you at the altar to provide the fire needed for your offering.

> I appeal to you therefore, brothers, by the mercies of God, to present your bodies as a living sacrifice, holy and acceptable to God, which is your

49

spiritual worship.

- Romans 12:1 (ESV)

I remember a teaching I heard about asking God to bring fire on one's offering. Whatever desire, calling, character or hope we aspire to in our Christian walk, we should ask God to cleanse with fire. When flames engulf these yearnings, *the true heart is exposed*. The dross burned away is our pretenses and we are left with *the purest form of our longing*. Our desire towards Him only comes from Him and results in being like Him. Thus we become a living sacrifice.

I wish I could have identified my pretense of pride and super-woman attempts prior to humiliating myself before my boss and co-workers. Although it hurt to feel weak, a painfully glorious season began in my life. His presence and provision of fiery challenges exposed the dross of my heart and led me to a sincere sacrifice – one of humility and grace. Give thanks for fiery times, because our God is faithful to salt you with fire.

FOR FURTHER THOUGHT.....

You know the stories, people and circumstances that left you hurt and struggling. What was God cultivating in you through these specific situations?

How can the challenges you have endured result in a more powerful testimony?

[*un*•earth]

en•d*ea*v•or [en'devər]

verb
[intrans.] to do one's utmost; be at pains; strive,
aspire, or struggle to achieve something.

[*un*•earth]

THE *most* EXCELLENT WAY

Our media, music and culture have taught us that love is: flirting, passion, ecstasy, attraction and incredible sex. This is *quite* a different list than what we find in 1 Corinthians 13. Love is described there as being kind, patient, forgiving one another, holding no record of wrongs, hoping and trusting. Seriously, that first list sounds much more intriguing, yet it will leave us empty. The fullness of love is not found in those things alone. Love is not only something solely to be given; as a child of God, it is a part of who you are. It is all-inclusive, from the stranger in the grocery store to your roommate and your parents. Love can be offered in any relationship. To embark on a journey towards excellence, love must become a conscious choice in every decision we make.

LOVING ON THE FIELD

I remember the insomnia of one night in the Dominican Republic. I was physically and emotionally exhausted, but my mind was racing and my heart felt heavy. I had been working only two months with at-risk teenagers, and was responsible to supervise one girl who was a habitual cutter. I was in the room next to hers and could not turn down the volume of her pain that seeped under the door. I wanted to be close, to try to help. I rose from my attempts of sleep to "guard" the door. I could not help but acknowledge and take action against the enemy's endeavors to steal, kill and destroy. There was a battle over this young woman's freedom and joy, and the Lord had just mobilized me to fight for her as she slept. I prayed, cried and spoke snippets of scripture through the night. Had I taken the common sense route, and gotten my much-needed sleep, I would have missed the pain and passion of His heart for this girl I barely knew but He cared for so intimately.

Authentically engaging our hearts with others is a relentless battle to love. To pray for this girl was not only a glorious invitation but also an act of obedience. In my missions experience, I have learned that love is entering into the pain as well as the glory of this world. There is no way to love authentically without getting messy. And messes will surely erupt as broken people collide in their pursuit to be like Christ. When I think of great lovers in this world, I think of people who endured heartache and struggle in their efforts to love well. These people are people who give of themselves without expectation or restraint, to love without return. We could list icon lovers: Mother Theresa, Gandhi, and the Apostle Paul, but these seem too lofty. Picture for one moment someone in your life who has loved you well. A person who has encouraged you, believed in you, and been faithful to you…. does anyone come to your mind?

The value of true love from someone is priceless. This is the reason the Bible specifies the greatest of faith, hope, and love……is love.

> And now I will show you the most
> excellent way.
> > - 1 Corinthians 12:31b

After spending a whole chapter instructing the church on spiritual gifting, Paul says, "now I will show you the most excellent way" which leads into 1 Corinthians 13, the chapter on love. Paul reiterates his point again: even if I know every language, have all wisdom, faith to heal, give all I have to those in need, but fail to love, it counts as nothing. Nothing. Your every dollar and every effort overseas is in vain if you have not done it with love. If we serve an un-reached people group but are jealous and unkind to teammates, it counts as nothing. We may raise thousands of dollars to spend two weeks overseas, but if we do not pray for and give to missions throughout the rest of the year, we are failing to love wholly. Keep in mind, the mission field is not only overseas – there are international students, compassion projects, refugee and homeless shelters in every city. There are lost people in need all around you. The most excellent way is not the mission field itself; it is the love you choose to walk in every day of your life.

This is a calling of excellence: to enter into something that will take the breath out of you. Love will at times sting deeper and ache more than you think you can bear. Although it demands so much of you, it is the most heavenly gift we can engage in here on earth. Above all, love calls you to lay down your life and will for someone else. As Mother Teresa held dying children in her arms she realized something few of us understand, our ache to be loved is healed through the loving of another. Christ's greatest act of love was giving

Himself for each of us. In His expression, we
have been given the remedy to the cravings of
this world....sacrificial love. When we offer
ourselves to the widows, our teammates, the poor,
and our family, we are one step closer to truly
understanding what love is, thus, a little closer to
the most excellent way.

LOVING AT HOME

We may feel lost when we return home because
loving others appears different than it was
overseas. Love is harder to express and interpret
in a culture that idolizes self-sufficiency. Looking
at the physical aspect, when you were overseas,
you hugged and held more; you served and gave
of yourself. You were in a setting that required
all of you: mentally, spiritually and emotionally.
It is nearly impossible to recreate the way you
gave and felt love on the mission field. Upon
return, home no longer feels as satisfying. The
everyday opportunities to give of yourself feel
more ambiguous and less effective. You may feel

a larger disconnect in the way you engage life here in the states. Your interaction with hurting and lost people is no longer as apparent.

In the midst of poverty and need, a life of love can be more tangibly demonstrated. When we return home, we are not as quickly motivated by our surroundings. It is not as easy to move towards loving people well. We have conditioned ourselves to believe it is greater to love in third world and desolate cultures than in our own neighborhood. Our eyes have become calloused to seeing the needs in everyone at home. Yet hurting people are all around us. Satan has fooled us. Everyday, our spiritual battle to love is right before us.

LOVING FROM A BROKEN CISTERN

> *For my people have committed two evils: they have forsaken me, the fountain of living waters, and hewed out cisterns for themselves, broken cisterns that can hold no water.*
>
> *- Jeremiah 2:13*

61

So, how do I love if I am an imperfect person? How do I give of myself when I am hurt and broken? We were never made to love within our own power. We are broken cisterns and we spend most of our time and energy trying to keep enough "water" to sustain ourselves. God knew this and that is why He tells us to stay near the living water. We must be ever renewed by Him if we are going to love others well. If Christ's love is the only thing that can truly sustain and fulfill you, then how can we ever love apart from it? God tells us our broken cisterns can hold no water; we must come to Him to provide.

What does loving from a broken cistern look like?

You must learn to give of yourself even though the outcome may not be as fulfilling. You were accepted and appreciated overseas and you are now fighting to love in a very independent culture. How do you give from yourself, how do you love other people if you feel alone, selfish, or lost? What would it look like to love from this messiness, offering others your heart, unabashed and muddled?

The answer is to live offering *authenticity*.

We live in a veneer culture that masks raw pain. People fear living from truth and loving out of their struggle and hurt. It is not until we push through and taste the freedom of living an illuminated life that we know grace and can find healing, community, and worship. You must not forsake the living water. We are not giving you formulaic methods because the process is unique for each person. Great acts of worship come in the midst of hardship, and in the same way love is most powerful when offered from an authentic heart. The most excellent way is a journey we each take to embrace who we are and love out of our heart, a broken cistern.

[*un*•earth]

FOR FURTHER THOUGHT....

How will you give from yourself, how will you love other people if you feel alone, selfish, or lost?

What would it look like to love from this messiness, offering others your heart, unabashed and muddled?

Are you living in authenticity even now in answering these questions? Whom will you be honest and vulnerable with?

How did you demonstrate love on your trip? When did you struggle to love? How well did you love? How could that love be translate back home?

[*un*•earth]

as•sim•i•l*ate* [ə'simə,lāt]

verb
[trans.] to bear a resemblance; integrate, absorb
or ingest.

[*un*•earth]

EXCESS *meets* SCARCITY

Walking into an airport after living overseas will send anyone into a little culture shock. Upon first entry we are bombarded with busyness, cell phones, and the noise of our own language. People are rushing by and around you with little, if any, social dialogue or emotional connection. Expect to be overwhelmed while grocery shopping in the cereal aisle or trying to choose from 114 types of toothpaste. **Our culture is over-stimulated by the amount of options we have.**

Decaf or regular? Email or text? Silver, gold, white gold, or platinum? Fat-free, soy or whole milk? Class online or campus? Yellow, green, purple or white cauliflower? Paper-back, hard-back, leather or engraved? Organic, cage-free, or Omega-3?

It will be hard to jump from a culture of simplicity back into a mentality of surplus. When excess meets scarcity there is little room to find an in between. It is similar to the tension you feel when walking out of a downtown restaurant and encountering a homeless person. Can you sense the pull of two conflicting life circumstances? The same conflict will meet you after a mission trip. The enemy would want you to forget the truths you so blatantly encountered. The things overseas you were sure you would never forget now threaten to become lost incentives. Engage in the tension; it will allow you to process re-entry in a more healthy way.

EXCESS IS NOT THE ENEMY

After a trip from Africa, life immediately went right back to where I had left it: studying, work, friends, responsibilities and church. *I am adjusting just fine to the reverse culture shock they told me I would encounter.* I had spoken too soon. I had been home about two weeks, settling into my Starbucks routine, when a drive-thru customer turned into a lesson in culture shock for me. She ordered a very specialized drink which filled each box on her cup, including the specific degrees of her latte. She immediately handed her beverage back to me, stating it was not the temperature she wanted. Trained as I am in great customer service, I did not hesitate a moment and remade her order. It was the second time she handed it back that I flickered with frustration. Before she could even tell me what was wrong I spouted, "Ma'am, I just spent the last two weeks in Africa feeding starving orphans and it is really hard for me to understand what you could possibly need right now."

She did not say a word, put a twenty-dollar bill in the tip box and drove away.

You might think she deserved my judgment; then let this be a lesson for you as it was for me. This was a perfect opportunity to find a balance between the contentions of two different worlds. We find our home culture idolizes excess and we visit places of scarcity. We feel a pull inside to try to bring together the two extremes we are experiencing. If we press into the tension of these moments, we will find opportunities to lessen the gap. Use every occasion to allow your heart to stay in touch with **both worlds**.

I was in the grocery store shopping for a family camping trip with my sister, less than two months of being home from Lithuania. Four hundred dollars later, I am mumbling criticisms under my breath as I unloaded the groceries into the house. *It is camping...you catch fish and start fire with flint...four hundred dollars? This is ridiculous.* I was upset for most of the camping trip. I could not let go of the money issue. After seeing people with so little, I became frustrated with spending so much. You also might find yourself critical towards materialism, but excess is not the enemy.

One more time because this is the key, **excess is not the enemy.**

An attitude of gratefulness is what guards us from either extreme – judging the wealth or fearing the poverty. Whether it is little or much, we acknowledge and are thankful that all belongs to God. Your money, time, education and all that you may earn or inherit are only **vessels of stewardship**. Your car, your spouse, your home, your computer, your ethnicity, your assets, and your friends are all vessels. They all belong to Him..

> He owns the cattle on a thousand hills.
> - Psalms 50:10

That verse never really moved me. I thought,

wonderful, God owns everything, which is great. It was not until I moved to Texas; I realized there are a lot of cows! I was driving back to college after a visit home and I was crying over finances and family issues. The sunset over the hill illuminated hundreds of cattle grazing in the fields. For miles as I drove, all I could see were black silhouettes like polka dots covering acres of land. This scene resounded: His grandeur - He owns everything. The verse came to me; *He owns the cattle on a thousand hills.*

God owns everything. Which simply means, it is not yours. You are simply a steward of it; you are more or less borrowing from God. We will have to give an account to how we took care of His property. This thought leaves me questioning, *how have I cared for His creation, His children?* In light of His sovereignty, everything we have must be weighed in humility. This invites us to explore our culture's struggle with materialism.

Picture materialism as a smokescreen. It is woven

deeply into our present day lives and we can either be consumed by it or turned off by it. When we press into the tension, God invites us to experience more aspects of Him; possibly, things about Him we might not even like or understand. This progression is painful but beautiful. God has entrusted us with an opportunity to engage in His heart. He is allowing us to see new sides of Him and His glory in order that we can reflect His global magnificence - to feel and live in a way few dare to live.

We encourage you to prayerfully navigate through these places of tension. This is not about legalism or rules, but the grace of God's specific plan for each of us. After seeing people without shoes or families sleeping five to a bed, how will you live differently? **There is a *balance* between the humility of scarcity and the peace within excess.** We encourage you to explore with an open heart how God might stretch you in this area. Whether it is fasting from your bed, cell phone, internet or a meal, going on prayer walks or volunteering at a shelter - how are you being faithful with the little things and the big things? These questions must come out of a heart that is burdened for others. Your return will offer you an opportunity to live radically. Ask Him what it looks like to cultivate a heart that is more globally minded.

You may find yourself on either side of the pendulum, perfectly fine with your transition home. You may feel great about where God has you with all that you own or possibly you feel guilt for coming home at all. You may begin to question: why am I paying for school when there are people starving, why am I ministering in a Western church when there is a lost world? There are millions of questions that will come to your mind, multiple convictions that you will face. **Take each of them to the Lord.** He was specific to make you with your personality and uniqueness. What is He asking of you? How are you to live? Is your ministry here in America? Is it overseas? Is it to support missions financially or prayerfully? Is it something different than everyone else? God has a reason He is putting all of this on your heart. Follow His leading.

[*un*•earth]

FOR FURTHER THOUGHT.....

What did you learn on the field that you want to apply to your everyday life?

Our everyday lives are not lived in high drama. Normal daily life is not doing relief work, but do you know where the orphanages are in your community?

We spend once a year raising all this support to go on a mission trip and never touch the mission field any other time. Looking at your finances (however small they are) could you give to the church, a country, organization, or sponsored child overseas?

[*un*•earth]

tr*ans*•fig•ure [trans'figyər]

verb
[trans.] to change so as to glorify or exalt,
transform.

[*un*•earth]

A *lasting* IMPACT

Two and a half weeks after the storm hit, our
team drove into the destroyed communities on
the Gulf coast. We went house to house tearing
down sheetrock, pulling out floors and removing
flooded appliances. To keep the horrific stench
tolerable, we put two breathing masks together
with orange peels between them – which I later
deemed the best invention on our trip. Through
mold, maggots and mud we searched the remains
of devastated homes.

For me, the most heartbreaking discovery was yet to come. Four miles from our work site was my family lodge, a home we have taken trips to since I was a small child. My heart quickened as we drove down the familiar roads. Many houses I knew by memory were now strewn over slabs of foundation. Perhaps my fears would not be true and our home would be salvageable. Turning the corner, I was no longer the relief worker but the victim. The frame of the house was torn, leaving the kitchen and living room exposed. I tried to coach myself, *this is only a structure*, but I could not fool my heart.

As our team searched through the remains, we decided to yell "Treasure!" every time we found something of worth. I was digging through the insulation and broken glass when I found an old photo album. The first page I wiped off was a picture of my sister and me as young teenagers with goofy hats on. The tears came, "Treasure!" I yelled through the sobs, "Treasure!".

At dusk, we sat in the driveway, sorting through what the world would consider worthless trinkets. I looked at the small pieces of my past and realized that being part of this family is the true treasure. My legacy runs so much deeper than material possessions. My family and my inheritance are a part of who I am. It is the same way for those who belong to the family of God; the real treasure is not what we have, but who we are because of Him. As believers, we do not have to fear the devastation of land, home, family and friends. We may have to mourn it, but we do not have to fear it. Though the loss of these things may rip us apart, we have a foundation and legacy in the family of God. This is our true treasure.

A REDEEMED INHERITANCE

Our inheritance is secured in our salvation. When God made you His child, He gave you access to the kingdom. Whether we come from a broken, dysfunctional home or struggle with the addictions and lies of this world, we have been

85

adopted into a family, a holy priesthood. What has been stolen from you in this present world has been redeemed through Christ's blood. If it is your identity, your peace, your virginity or your family, God has paid the price for redemption. He longs for you to run in perseverance and freedom; perseverance in faith that He is a good Father and in the freedom that you are sealed in Him.

> Then the King will say to those on his right, 'Come, you who are blessed by my Father; *take your **inheritance**,* the kingdom prepared for you since the creation of the world.
> - Matthew 25:34, emphasis added

This inheritance, knowing who you are, will lead to a legacy of lasting impact. Whether you choose never to go overseas again or you become a full-time missionary in Guam, you are called to leave an impact however you live. Leaving a legacy requires you to live authentically; **authenticity requires vulnerability and perseverance.** Don't expect the world, or even your friends, to applaud this radical way of life. They will, however, notice and be drawn to the passion you emanate. This genuine living can only be done well through knowing who you are, which is the gift of your inheritance. Though each story is different, the reason we can stand in this world with hope is because we have all been given a new name, a new life. We are all children of the King.

If you come home from overseas and your life feels turned upside down, embrace it. If you feel different and the things you were certain about are now unstable, this is typical. It is as if the filing cabinet of your values, spirituality and goals has been dumped on the floor, and you are in the middle of a scattered mess of yourself. How do you organize the files? Will they all fit? Which files go in the front or the back? Will you throw any out?

As we have encouraged you to delve further, we realize you will burn out if you are not secure in the foundation of who you are in Christ. Do not go there if you have not established a solid foundation. The deeper you go into your God-authored story the more struggle you will find, and thus, the more glory you will find. When you come home to engage in the world around you, love well from an illuminated life. Invite your community to walk next to you in this journey. To be truly alive is to stand secure in who God has fashioned you to be. Ask for help, we need each other.

LEAVING YOUR LEGACY

After combining our 21 mission trips, we want to know if we are living any different. Have we left a legacy or simply found a way to check off another box to an adventurous, spiritual life?

We keep reminding ourselves the lifestyle we lead and legacy we desire to leave is so much larger than our location. God is teaching us there is an opportunity to be an offering every moment of every day. These moments may seem small yet they are purposeful choices to love well. Helping your roommate with the dishes can be just as loving as ministering to Chinese college students.

Afghanistan. San Diego. Peru. Jackson. Indonesia. Orlando.
Love well.
Widows. Parents. Prostitutes. Friends. Gypsies.
Love well.

With every challenge we have addressed and all the endeavors of the process, our hope would be to send you out to live an extreme and crazy life. Meaning we desire for you to live in a way few dare. You may feel as if you come off this high-drama and intensely spiritual trip crashing into an ordinary life. This is not true. **Your life is not mundane if everyday is purposeful.**

How does the changed you look in a familiar place?

How will you make radical decisions in a seemingly ordinary life?

[*un*•earth]

How do you not fall back into the person you were before?

Will you fight to live out of the inheritance of your calling rather than choosing what the world offers?

Be honest in the way you live. Embrace the emotional and spiritual place God is inviting you into. Love others to a new depth, knowing it will be the most fulfilling and challenging gift you can give or receive. See the fire in your life as a salting; look for new maps that blow your existing paradigms. There is so much beauty in this invitation. This calling is what we believe is the journey God has begun in you, one with a lasting impact.

> The LORD bless you and keep you;
> The LORD make his face shine upon you and be gracious to you;
> The LORD turn his face toward you and give you peace.
>
> - Numbers 6:24-26

[*un*•earth]

[*un*•earth]

Etched in the wall of Mother Teresa's Calcutta home
for the sick are these words...

People are often unreasonable, irrational, and self-centered.
Forgive them anyway.
If you are kind, people may accuse you of selfish ulterior motives.
Be kind anyway.
If you are successful you will win some unfaithful friends and
some genuine enemies.
Succeed anyway.
If you are honest and sincere, people may deceive you.
Be honest and sincere anyway.
What you spend years creating, others could destroy overnight.
Create anyway.
If you find serenity and happiness some may be jealous.
Be happy anyway.
The good you do today will often be forgotten.
Do good anyway.
Give the best you have, it will never be enough.
Give your best anyway.
In the final analysis, it is between you and God.
It was never between you and them anyway.

[*un*•earth]

ACKNOWLEDGEMENTS
and Thanks

We appreciate the following for their support and commitment:

To my 'Jonathan', for your sacrifice and love. There are no words to describe the depth of my gratefullness.

Tom Vidrine (DeeDarling) for housing two aspiring authors as they wrote!

Kinsey Kroeger for her hours of design and creativity.

Plethora Publishing for taking on our book.

Steve Kessler for pastoral coverage.

Matt Bartley for painstakingly revising our theology.

Our mothers, Christine Anthony and Janet Rogers, for proofing, prayers and encouragement. (And looking back on it, we think breastfeeding was a wise decision.)

Toni and Angie: Sunday night with you got us here.

Crystal, Lauri, Jenni, Bonnie, Tom, Sarah, Jody and everyone else we made read this prior to printing!

Thank you!

[*un*•earth]

[*un*•earth]

[*un*•earth]